101

WAYS

TO HAVE A

GREAT DAY AT WORK

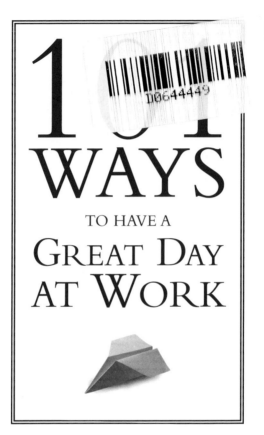

STEPHANIE GODDARD DAVIDSON

SOURCEBOOKS, INC.®
NAPERVILLE, ILLINOIS

Published by Sourcebooks, Inc.
P.O. Box 4410, Naperville, Illinois 60567–4410
(630) 961–3900
Fax: (630) 961–2168
www.sourcebooks.com

ISBN-13: 978-1-4022-0779-2
ISBN-10: 1-4022-0779-4

Printed and bound in the United States of America.
CH 10 9 8 7 6 5 4 3 2

DEDICATION

To my husband Bill—who has given me a perfect life.

- -

ACKNOWLEDGMENTS

I would like to thank my agent Sheree Bykofsky and my editor Deb Werksman, who both said "yes" and then worked hard to make this book happen.

I would also like to thank that part of the Universe that gives you an idea for a book; then stays close by while you write it; taps the right people on the shoulder to help you; effortlessly.

INTRODUCTION

Are you having a bad day at work—again? Often, in the midst of all there is to do, and all the stresses of the workplace, it's hard to remember that you have some control, some power, over how your day goes.

This book provides you with simple tips and techniques for making positive changes in your current position. Whether you read straight through and work one technique per day, or whether you dip into the book as needed, you will find you can actually make an impact on your circumstances and have a great day at work no matter what's happening.

Having spent many years counseling and training employees and managers who are unhappy in their jobs, I have based my entire career on showing others how to have a great day at work. I have personally and professionally read hundreds of books on business, interpersonal relations, and self-help.

This extensive reading has influenced my approach to solving the problems that are common in the workplace. The training manuals that I have created have been used successfully by many Fortune 100 companies. My promise to you is, if you apply the suggestions in this book, you'll have a renewed sense of purpose in your job and the tools to make every day a great day.

To have meaningful work is a tremendous happiness.

—RITA MAE BROWN

1
Make a list

Reflect back to the time you accepted your position. What were the aspects of this job that were important to you then? Try to remember how excited you were about these.

Now list ten reasons why you still like your job. Keep this list where you will come across it occasionally. When you do come across it, stop what you are doing and read it.

Set me a task in which I can put something of my very self, and it is a task no longer; it is joy; it is art.

—BLISS CARMAN

2

Set more than just goals

Write down five things you would really like to see happen to you this year. Make sure these cover physical, social, romantic, career, and spiritual areas. File this list in a thirty-day file that you can refer to every month to check your progress.

Hard work spotlights the character of people: some turn up their sleeves, some turn up their noses, and some don't turn up at all.

—SAM EWING

3

Get it out of the way

Do the things you dislike most about your job first. Then reward yourself by doing the things you like best about your job.

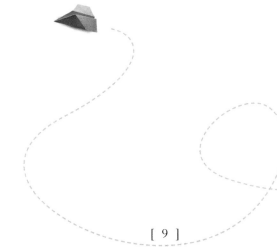

The higher the pay in enjoyment the worker gets out of it, the higher shall be his pay in money also.

—MARK TWAIN

4

Maximize your salary

Determine one thing you can do to make better use of your salary this year (e.g., start a 401K, increase the percentage you already contribute to your 401K, cut down by half how often you go out to eat). If you are already on a solid financial path, or if you are known to be a little too frugal, now figure out one way you can also reward yourself financially each payday. A special dinner, a massage, a new plant. Just make sure the money is spent on you.

Positive attitude—optimism, high self-esteem, an outgoing nature, joyousness, and the ability to cope with stress—may be the most important bases for continued good health.

—HELEN HAYES

5

Do something healthy

Do one thing today that you consider "healthy." It may be skipping that mid-afternoon candy bar or taking a walk at lunch hour. Or maybe just fastening your seatbelt on the way home. Whatever you choose, don't discount it as too easy or silly. You have just sent a message to your subconscious that you are valuable.

You don't have to buy from anyone. You don't have to work at any particular job. You don't have to participate in any given relationship. You can choose.

—HARRY BROWNE

6

Plan by relationships, not by the hour

Try planning today by the relationships that are most important to you, instead of by schedules or deadlines. Everything we do is really just a reflection of the relationships we have with others or with ourselves. Schedule at least two of these relationships into your day.

No man ever listened himself out of a job.

—Calvin Coolidge

7
Listen up

Make a conscious effort today to listen more than you speak.

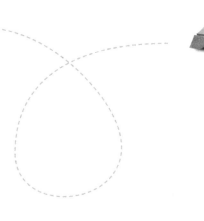

I take responsibility for the air I breathe and the space I take up. I try to be immediate, to be totally present for all my work.

—Maya Angelou

8

Breathe

Notice your breathing all day. When you find that you have forgotten to do this, take three slow, deep, gentle breaths and start again.

*Those people who develop
the ability to continuously acquire
new and better forms of
knowledge that they can apply to
their work and to their lives will
be the movers and shakers in our
society for the indefinite future.*

—BRIAN TRACY

9

Learn something new

Decide that every person that you come in contact with today can teach you something. Be aware of this possibility and manage the conversation toward this outcome.

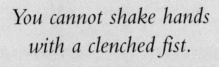

You cannot shake hands with a clenched fist.

—INDIRA GANDHI

10

Mend fences

Consider a relationship at work in which you are dissatisfied (we all have one). Schedule a conversation that will address the issue. Throughout this process, consider where you have some responsibility for the condition of this relationship.

Time is the coin of your life.
It is the only coin you have,
and only you can determine
how it will be spent.
Be careful lest you let other
people spend it for you.

—CARL SANDBURG

11

Do what you can

It's easy to see what's not possible. The hard part is seeing what can be done. Is someone or something holding you back? Turn your attention today to the things you can control and do something about them.

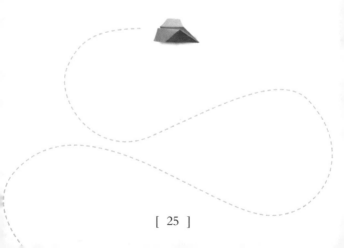

The most important single ingredient in the formula of success is knowing how to get along with people.

—THEODORE ROOSEVELT

12

Let it all hang out

The next time you are really angry with a coworker write a "rage" letter. Really let it all out. When you are done, make sure it is completely destroyed. You will feel better. If you don't, write another and another until you do.

In today's environment,
hoarding knowledge
ultimately erodes your power.
If you know something
very important, the way
to get power is by
actually sharing it.

—JOSEPH BADARACCO

13

Share your knowledge

What are a couple of things you know you are good at in your job? Write these down. Now, think of a population in your company that would benefit from having this information. Create an outline for a presentation, an informal training, or even just a brown bag lunch-and-learn. (Use hand-outs only as a last resort.) Don't worry about your presentation skills. You are the expert sharing this information.

What you share is important, not how you share it. Take full responsibility for planning the presentation and carrying it through, checking with your boss and anyone else in the company who may be interested.

The way you treat yourself sets the standard for others.

—Sonya Friedman

14

Treat yourself

Buy yourself flowers and keep them on your desk. Or, consider buying yourself the perfect writing instrument, a small fishbowl and fish, or a plant.

The positive thinker sees the invisible, feels the intangible, and achieves the impossible.

—Anonymous

15

Stay positive

Try to say nothing negative or judgmental all day. You won't be able to do it, but try anyway.

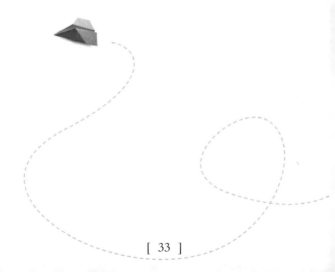

The important thing about a problem is not its solution, but the strength we gain in finding the solution.

—ANONYMOUS

16

Be part of the solution

Take a look at areas of your job where there are problems, or there's something missing. Then, come up with realistic "fixes" for these. If you cannot come up with a solution, move on. Focusing on impossible goals wastes your energy and creates unnecessary stress. Share your solutions with someone who can help you implement them. Even if nothing changes, you'll be seen as someone who is trying to affect the workplace constructively.

During [these] periods of relaxation after concentrated intellectual activity, the intuitive mind seems to take over and can produce the sudden clarifying insights which give so much joy and delight.

—FRITJOF CAPRA

17

Change the scenery

Take a few minutes to go to a different floor, a different bathroom, or some other area where you rarely visit. If you can, take a few minutes there to slow down, breathe, or just sit quietly.

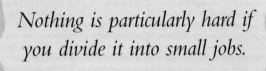

Nothing is particularly hard if you divide it into small jobs.

—HENRY FORD

18

Take it one thing at a time

Concentrate on doing one thing at a time today. Stop multitasking. Notice how long it takes you to get your job done today versus the days you normally do more than one thing at the same time. After you note that there is little difference in your productivity, take a look at your stress level at the end of the day.

To praise others for their virtues can but encourage one's own efforts.

—THOMAS PAINE

19

Pass the word

The next time someone goes above and beyond for you, tell that person's boss.

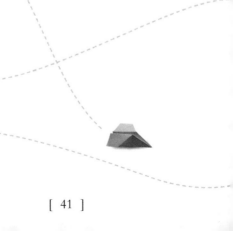

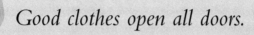

Good clothes open all doors.

—THOMAS FULLER

20

Dress for success

If something you wear to work makes you feel too fat, too thin, too old, or just not your best—get rid of it. Even if you are on a tight wardrobe budget, it's not worth it. Your work is affected by your self-image. You really only need five outfits. No one notices or cares how many outfits you own, just as long as you don't wear the same thing twice in a week.

Inspiration exists, but it has to find us working.

—PABLO PICASSO

21
Find inspiration

Find a quote that really inspires you and post it somewhere prominent in your workspace. Even better, find a role model in your field, and read up on how he or she achieved success.

It's not the hours you put in your work that counts, it's the work you put in the hours.

—SAM EWING

22

Take it easy

If someone tells you that you are working too much, believe it, and consider slowing down.

No kind action ever stops with itself.
One kind action leads to another.
Good example is followed. A single
act of kindness throws out roots in
all directions, and the roots spring up
and make new trees. The greatest
work kindness does to others is that
it makes them kind themselves.

—Amelia Earhart

23
Build a bridge

If there is an employee, coworker, or manager with whom you have some tension, take the first step and try to remedy it. Our success is only measured by the quality of our relationships. The results we get at work are directly tied to this fundamental truth.

Any effort you make toward making the relationship better will not go unnoticed, even if it appears to at first.

*Ninety percent of
the friction of daily life
is caused by tone of voice.*

—Arnold Bennett

24
Notice your voice

Notice the quality and volume of your voice. Too soft? Too loud? Too high? Voice quality is a crucial part of how we communicate. Focus on how you use your voice today. Think of it as an instrument. When do you need to soft-pedal? When does increasing the volume help? When does it harm?

*Motivation is everything.
You can do the work of
two people, but you can't be
two people. Instead, you have
to motivate the next guy
down the line and get him
to inspire his people.*

—LEE IACOCCA

25

Ask about motivation

If you have employees, ask them to list four or five things that really motivate them. This can be done in a staff meeting, via email, or one-on-one. If you do not have employees, decide four or five things that really motivate you. Let your manager know what these are in a way that is positive and helpful. Approach this as a "group effort" to making the most of your contribution. Most importantly, don't assume you know what motivates others or that they know what motivates you.

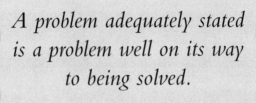

*A problem adequately stated
is a problem well on its way
to being solved.*

—R. Buckminster Fuller

26

What's the problem?

You will get better results from thoroughly defining a problem before you try to solve it. The famous educator Thomas Dewey once said, "A problem well-defined is half solved." Don't jump into a solution. Focus on the problem or issue first. Make sure you have all the facts. Then, get down to the business of fixing it.

If you are seeking creative ideas, go out walking. Angels whisper to a man when he goes for a walk.

—RAYMOND INMON

27

Walk around

Walk around at a convenient time for you each day. Talk with the people that you need to before they find you. Make a regular practice of "managing by walking around." You'll have a lot more time for the things you need to do—more than you ever dreamed. People will feel your presence without the need to communicate through emails, unscheduled visits, or meetings.

To be a success, devote three or four hours a day to being an executive and the rest of the time to thinking.

—FELIX FRANKFURTER

28

Sit and think

There is nothing wrong with taking time to just sit and think. Sometimes our society views sitting and thinking as being nonproductive. Most Eastern cultures actually schedule parts of the day where they stop what they are doing and think. In the words of author Sylvia Boorstein, "Don't just do something; sit there!"

The more we give to others,
the more we are increased.

—Lao Tzu

29

Give an award

Create some kind of gift or award for someone you have been ignoring due to your workload. Make sure you communicate the reason for the gift.

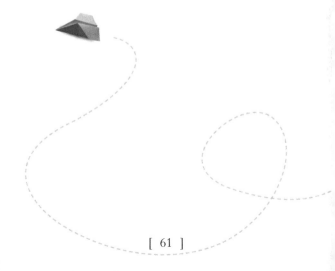

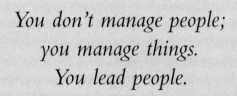

*You don't manage people;
you manage things.
You lead people.*

—GRACE MURRAY HOPPER

30

Empower others

When someone comes to you with a problem, focus on empowering that person to come up with a solution. By being the problem-solver you end up taking responsibility for the outcome. Instead, let the person "own" the problem and the solution. You'll have more time for your own problems and will have encouraged a coworker to work independently of you.

*I like people to come back
and tell me what
I did wrong. That's the
kindest thing you can do.*

—LILLIAN GISH

31
Keep it work-related

The next time you feel you need to give someone criticism, decide on how this comment specifically relates to his or her performance. If it doesn't, you may be judging by style and how it differs from yours instead of a true work concern. If it does relate to work, find a way to present it that focuses on the facts only, not on personality or style.

If you want to leave your footprints on the sand of time, be sure you're wearing work shoes.

—ITALIAN PROVERB

32
Take responsibility

You are completely responsible for where you are in your career. To blame others is to give them your power. Instead, put that energy into taking the actions you need to get the job you want. Do at least one thing every day that gets you closer to that goal—no matter how small that action may seem.

When love and skill work together, expect a masterpiece.

—JOHN RUSKIN

33

Love your work

Theodore Roosevelt said, "Far and away, the best prize that life offers is the chance to work hard at work worth doing." Are you making career decisions based on money? Or title? Consider the words above. Money and title don't get you very far when you are miserable eight hours a day.

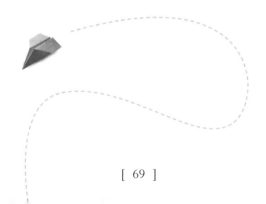

Does a smile help business?
Try it. Joy makes
the face shine, and he that
hath a merry heart hath
a continual feast.

—W. C. ISETT

34
Smile

Do you smile at work? If not, you may be confusing your serious look with professionalism. The reality is that not smiling just makes you appear unhappy.

Never write on a subject without first having read yourself full on it; and never read on a subject till you have thought yourself hungry on it.

—JEAN PAUL RICHTER

35

Read up!

Do you subscribe to any of your industry's or profession's publications? Even just browsing through these magazines, books, and newspapers will provide you with enough information to offer new and progressive ideas to your workplace. And others will start seeing you as someone who is leading, not following.

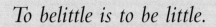

To belittle is to be little.

—ANONYMOUS

36
Feedback takes two

When you feel you must give someone constructive feedback (and this will
happen whether you manage others or
not) remember to ask the person his or
her opinion on the situation first. The
next step is to point out where you
both have similar positions on the
subject. Only then give one or two
suggestions that were not pointed out
by the person (if there are any). And,
remember to balance your constructive
feedback with some positive feedback
as well.

I am suggesting to you the simple idea that people work harder and smarter if they find their work satisfying and know that it is appreciated.

—ROBERT F. SIX

37

Give positive reinforcement

If you want behaviors repeated by your coworkers, tell them specifically what you liked. Don't just say, "Good job." Tell them what the behavior was and why it was important to you. This works for bosses, too!

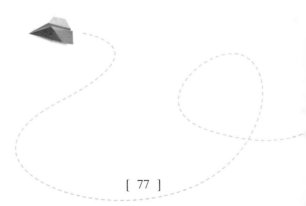

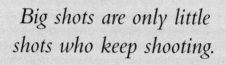

Big shots are only little shots who keep shooting.

—CHRISTOPHER MORLEY

38

Trust yourself

Trust that you have everything you need inside of you to make a decision. Even if the decision is "wrong" later, you will learn from it. There are no bad decisions, only better ones.

Success:
A process of becoming
who you already are.

—FRANK POTTS

39

You first!

The famous actress Katharine Hepburn said, "You learn in life that the only person you can really correct and change is yourself." Consider at least three things at work that you are trying to change. Now consider where you can modify your actions or thinking on these things.

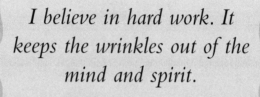

I believe in hard work. It keeps the wrinkles out of the mind and spirit.

—HELENA RUBINSTEIN

40

Thoughts are power

Stephen R. Covey quotes in his best-selling *Seven Habits of Highly Effective People*, "Reap a thought, sow an action. Reap an action, sow a habit. Reap a habit, sow a lifetime."

Pay attention to your thoughts today. They create your life.

Nothing is so fatiguing as the eternal hanging on of an uncompleted task.

—WILLIAM JAMES

41

Take ten!

The next time you can't get started on a task or project, tell yourself you will only work on it for ten minutes. Chances are you will stick with it once you've started, but even if you move on after ten minutes, you will have accomplished that much more.

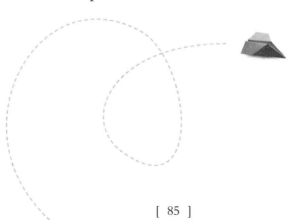

If you have a job
without aggravations,
you don't have a job.

—MALCOLM FORBES

42

Let it go

List the things that are really bugging you at work. Create as many things as you can. Get specific. What about the color of the carpet? The copy machines? The tie your boss is wearing today? Get out every drop of venom.

Now go back and read the list. See where you can do something about any of these. Also see where you simply cannot and let it go. (And don't forget to notice that little smile on your face at some of the items.)

If there is any great secret of success in life, it lies in the ability to put yourself in the other person's place and to see things from his point of view—as well as your own.

—HENRY FORD

43

Walk a mile in your boss' shoes

Sit quietly for a moment and imagine that you are your boss. Think about what his or her day is like, from the minute of arriving at the office to the walk outside at the end of the day.

What might it be like to have those responsibilities, to work for his or her boss? Walk in your boss' shoes. You will probably feel great relief that you have the job you do, and not the one your boss does!

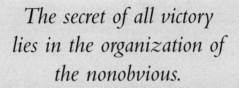

The secret of all victory
lies in the organization of
the nonobvious.

—MARCUS AURELIUS

44

Reorganize

Can you reorganize your office space? Sometimes just changing your files around, moving your desk, or hanging pictures differently can make a big difference.

How about bringing in pictures, art, keepsakes, fragrant oils, even music? If conditions don't allow you to decorate, look at what you can do to make your workspace yours, even if you must keep your personal objects hidden in a drawer.

The greatest gift is to give people your enlightenment, to share it.

—BUDDHA

45

Give a gift

Make today a day of giving gifts.
Not presents, but gifts. Where can you
help someone who is over-worked? Is
someone due a compliment? Does the
mailroom guy know that you notice
the accuracy and consistency of the
mail drop? Tell him. Find some way to
give a "gift" to every person with
whom you come in contact today.

Let us not look back in anger, nor forward in fear, but around in awareness.

—JAMES THURBER

46

Tune in

Stop what you are doing and notice your surroundings. Notice the chair you are sitting on (or how the floor feels if you are standing). Notice the color of the walls, the sounds you hear, the taste in your mouth. Try to sustain this awareness all day and see if your stress level goes down.

Besides the noble art of getting things done, there is a nobler art of leaving things undone…The wisdom of life consists in the elimination of the nonessentials.

—LIN YUTANG

47

Throw it out

Throw out any paperwork (with the exception of financial records) that has a date of two years or older, unless you absolutely can't part with it. If you feel this way about most items, consider that you may be holding onto unnecessary information. If it's something that important, you'll be able to get your hands on it again, even if you throw it out.

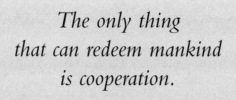

The only thing that can redeem mankind is cooperation.

—Bertrand Russell

48

Come up with win-win

Have you ever heard the term "win-win"? It's become a cultural icon. But what does it mean? Win-win means that there is always a better solution than compromise. Start thinking in these terms. Instead of giving in or forcing your position on another, try coming up with a completely different solution. It's possible, but only if you try.

*We are all created equal
with special gifts and if
we reach out to each other
in sharing these gifts,
we all become richer.*

—ROY HENRY VICKERS

49

Share your success strategies

Think about one or two things you do that contribute to your success and share them with someone else in an email, or tell someone about it over lunch. You'll be seen as someone who cares about other's success as well as your own—the true definition of a successful person.

*There are no mistakes,
no coincidences, all events
are blessings given to us
to learn from.*

—Elisabeth Kubler-Ross

50

No coincidences

The next time you are feeling unmotivated, try opening up this book to a random page. You'll probably find that you are reading exactly what you need right now.

The sum of wisdom is that time is never lost that is devoted to work.

—Ralph Waldo Emerson

51
Lose track of time

What is one activity that you do that makes you lose all track of time? Everyone has at least one thing like this. Pay attention to this phenomenon. Once you find it, see how you can create a job or career around it.

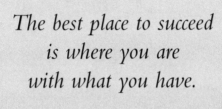

The best place to succeed
is where you are
with what you have.

—CHARLES M. SCHWAB

52

Take a look at your finances

How are your finances? Have you looked at your paycheck recently? I mean really looked at it? What deductions are you making, how much is going to taxes, where are you saving? Have you calculated the amount you pay in interest on your debt? Is it more than you have in stocks or savings? Sit down today and get familiar with your finances. They won't improve without attention. True financial security is getting a handle on your money. Only then can you make wise career choices.

To love what you do and feel that it matters—how could anything be more fun.

—KATHARINE GRAHAM

53

Love your work

What do you love about your job? Is it more than what you hate about it? Can the things you love be turned into work? Start thinking about this today.

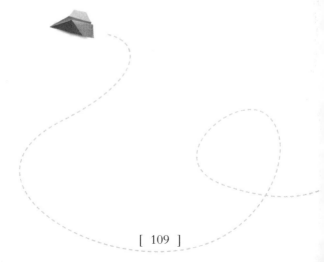

Life is 10 percent what happens to you and 90 percent how you react to it.

—Charles R. Swindoll

54

Notice reactions

Watch how much you react to today. To react means to let other people, circumstances, or other externals control you. When you notice you are reacting, stop and try another way. Even just noticing that you are about to react gives you a chance to respond with more power in the situation.

Do not keep away from the measure which has no limit, or from the task which has no end.

—RABBI TARPHON

55
Let it flow

When we try hard to do something, it is hard. When we just let things flow and roll with whatever comes our way, things start to work for us. Try expending the least effort today (this doesn't mean doing nothing; that's much harder than going with the flow).

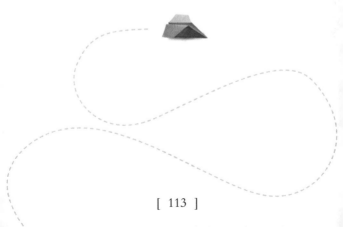

*There is only one way
to happiness, and that is
cease worrying about things
which are beyond the power
of our will.*

—EPICTETUS

56

Don't worry

Spending a lot of time feeling guilty or worrying? Guilt is giving attention to something that has passed. Worry is spending time thinking about something in the future. You don't have control over either, so stop wasting your time and increasing your stress.

Ask yourself what you can do right now about the situation. And then do it. Your guilt or worry will magically disappear.

The best thing about the future is that it comes only one day at a time.

—Abraham Lincoln

57
Create your future

What have you done to shape your future? If you haven't done much, it's time to get started. What do you want from your career? Take small steps, but start making it happen today.

Remember the two benefits of failure. First, if you do fail, you learn what doesn't work; and second, the failure gives you the opportunity to try a new approach.

—ROGER VON OECH

58

Take a risk

We lose out on a lot in life when we play it safe. Try being more courageous today. Even something small like introducing yourself to someone you have seen at work, but don't know, is a good step. The day will only get better.

If one advances confidently in the direction of his dreams, and endeavors to live the life he has imagined, he will meet with a success unexpected in common hours.

—Henry David Thoreau

59

Write a mission statement

If you do not have a mission statement, write one today. If you have one, get it out and review it. Make any changes to keep moving in the right direction. A mission statement should have your long-term goals at the forefront. Career, love, physical health, spirituality, important relationships, and mental challenge are areas to address.

Decide what you ultimately want to achieve in these areas and write it out. This is your mission statement.

Vision without action is a dream. Action without vision is simply passing time. Action with Vision is making a positive difference.

—JOEL BACKER

60

Visualize

Always plan with the end result in mind. If you are giving a presentation to a group of experts or just filing that stack of papers on your desk, don't start anything until you have visualized what you want. If you think this step isn't necessary, bear in mind that everything you do is a result of the mental picture you have of the end result. If you have a vague, half-hearted idea of what you want to accomplish, that is what you will get.

Be clear. Be specific.

Rise early. Work late.
Strike oil.

—J. PAUL GETTY

61

Go the extra mile

Give twice as much today as you normally do. Really go the extra mile. Instead of focusing on how much you have to do, or how little you get paid for it, give it all you've got just for today.

The happiest people seem to be those who have no particular reason for being so except that they are so.

—WILLIAM RALPH INGE

62

Be of service

To be of service to others can be a path to happiness. Where can you be of service to the people you work with?

Try looking at everything you do today as helping someone else instead of another checkmark on your to-do list.

The pitcher cries for water to carry and a person for work that is real.

—MARGE PIERCY

63

Drink water

Keep a full glass of water or a water bottle nearby and drink at least 8 oz. of water each morning and afternoon, especially if you're in a climate-controlled building. You might find yourself lessening your tendencies toward junk food snacks, cigarette breaks, or nail-biting, and you might have more energy.

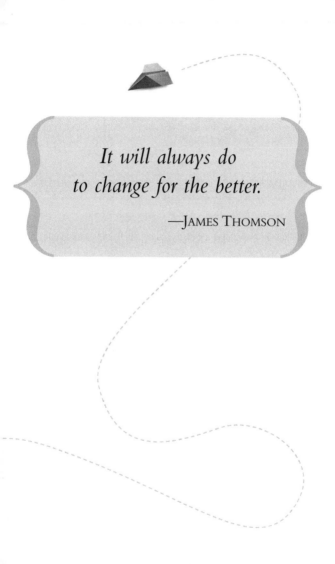

*It will always do
to change for the better.*

—JAMES THOMSON

64

Change your style

Try a completely different style today. If you are normally a "take charge" type, try emphasizing the part of you that can sit back and observe. If you normally hang in the background, assert your ideas today. Each of us has elements of every personality type; we just rely on one style predominately. Break out of your usual way and develop the rest of you.

*Character is the indelible
mark that determines
the only true value of all
people and all their work.*

—ORISON SWETT MARDEN

65

Build character

Instead of developing your personality, charm, or intellect, try exercising your character today. Character is the root; personality the flower. Your external "beauty" is only as strong as the roots no one can see.

The greatest remedy for anger is delay.

—SENECA

66

Take the sting out

The next time you are upset and are responding via email or through some other written correspondence, file it away for awhile and get out of there! Eat, get a soda, splash cold water on your face or wrists. Then go back and read your message. Alter the "jabs" and harsh wording. Then send it.

*Coming together is
a beginning; keeping
together is progress; working
together is success.*

—HENRY FORD

67

Work as a team

Management guru and author Harold Geneen says, "I don't believe in just ordering people to do things. You have to sort of grab an oar and row with them." Even if you don't directly manage others, you must manage your results through others. The next time you are about to give instructions or demand something from another, consider where you will "grab an oar."

*It is the province of
knowledge to speak and it
is the privilege of wisdom
to listen.*

—Oliver Wendell Holmes

68

Focus

While engaging in conversation today, focus on what the person is saying instead of formulating your reply. You'll know what to say when it's your turn.

Look around you—there are people around you. Maybe you will remember one of them all your life and later eat your heart out because you didn't make use of the opportunity to ask him questions. And the less you talk, the more you'll hear.

—ALEXANDER SOLZHENITSYN

69

Get to know others

If you are "low on the totem pole," start making plans to get to know the top executives in your company/workplace. Propose an idea or set up a meeting to get career guidance or advice on moving into something new. If you are a top executive, schedule time to get to know the frontline employees in the workplace. Spend a day in roundtables or familiarizing yourself with someone's routine. The knowledge and rewards of these actions will be unlimited.

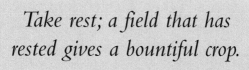

Take rest; a field that has rested gives a bountiful crop.

—Ovid

70
Renew

To be human is to be in constant renewal. We sleep to restore; we eat to re-energize; we shed cells daily to make room for new growth. Follow your body's lead and renew your work today. Throw out unnecessary clutter, try completing your tasks in a whole new way, think of something you would like to try or be involved in and figure out how to get it.

To get things done, we must work together. We must meet in the middle to work out our differences and find the best solutions.

—Christine Gregoire

71

Value your opposite

Think of the person at work who is most different from you. Consider five positive traits about this individual.

Open up to his or her contribution at work. If you draw a blank, get to know him or her better. Find what value this person provides.

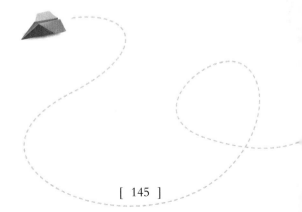

There is only one success—
to be able to spend your
own life in your own way.

—CHRISTOPHER MORLEY

72
Follow your bliss

If money and education were no object, what would you be doing for a living? If it's not what you are doing now, start planning. Can you create aspects of this career in your current situation? Can you volunteer your time to a charity that works in this area?

How about taking just one course in this area or talking with those who are doing this work? Life is short. Don't wait until later.

As we become ever more diverse, we must work harder to unite around our common values and our common humanity.

—BILL CLINTON

73
Put values first

You may read and hear through "pop psychology" that feelings are the most important aspect of yourself and must be expressed. But often this behavior does not serve you well. Put your values ahead of your feelings. The next time you are angry or worried or feeling guilty, think of the bigger issues to which you are committed, and act on these values, not on your feelings.

*As we grow as unique
persons, we learn to respect
the uniqueness of others.*

—ROBERT H. SCHULLER

74
Call people by their names

People respond in the deepest way to hearing their name. And one of the biggest insults is to forget a name or get someone's name wrong. Use people's names today as often as you can. If you are bad with names, try a memory trick like "Claire has lots of hair." Or write down the name and a characteristic that stands out to you.

Walking is good for the soul.

—Andrew A. Rooney

75

Take a walk

If the weather is bad, walk your stairs or corridors. Purposely walk to achieve your tasks today. Avoid calling by phone or letting the mailroom handle it. As you walk, focus on each step.

Conversation is an exercise of the mind; gossip is merely an exercise of the tongue.

—ANONYMOUS

76

Be loyal to the absent

When you gossip, you are demonstrating that you are untrustworthy. This not only compromises your credibility but undermines your relationships. Your value as a coworker will only multiply when you stop gossiping.

True leadership lies in guiding others to success. In ensuring that everyone is performing at their best, doing the work they pledged to do and doing it well.

—BILL OWENS

77
Hail to the chief!

The next time you can find only fault with your boss, reflect on his or her credentials, education, personality strengths, or political savvy. There is at least one good reason why he or she is in charge. If you can't find even one reason, you have to consider where you hold responsibility for this negative opinion.

*No matter how much
pressure you feel at work,
if you could find ways to
relax for at least
five minutes every hour,
you'd be more productive.*

—DR. JOYCE BROTHERS

78

Downtime is peaceful time

Use your "downtime" wisely. See it as a way to renew and recharge. Count your breaths or your blessings. Do this while standing in line or on a routine conference call. How about while watching TV or on the exercise bike? Use your time spent sitting in traffic as effective downtime.

*We can be sure that
the greatest hope for
maintaining equilibrium in
the face of any situation
rests within ourselves.*

—FRANCIS J. BRACELAND

79

Find your balance

Find a balance in your life so that the time you spend at work is more enjoyable. Make a list of the areas in your life to which you must dedicate your time (career, family, social life, spirituality, solitude, volunteer work, etc.) and prioritize your list.

Compare your priorities to how you currently spend most of your time. On which activity do you spend the smallest amount of time? The largest? Does this correspond with what you find important? This is the beginning point of finding balance in your life. You have to make choices. Decide how you will reconcile your two lists.

Without the meditative background that is criticism, works become isolated gestures, historical accidents, soon forgotten.

—MILAN KUNDERA

80

Take it in

The next time you receive criticism or feedback from someone about your work, consider these points:

- It's incredibly difficult to give someone feedback. The giver is more tense than you are.
- Without feedback, we never know what to change. It really is a gift.
- Recall feedback you have received in the past and recognize how valuable it eventually became.
- Try to find the areas with which you and the giver agree.
- People don't give feedback to be mean or judgmental. If they didn't care, they'd just let you fail.

Knowledge has to be improved, challenged, and increased constantly, or it vanishes.

—PETER F. DRUCKER

81

Sign up

Join a professional association. Find one that either suits your current profession or one into which you would like to move. If you don't think you have the time, consider that you don't have to go to every meeting or become an officer. The pay-off is information, contacts, ideas, job prospects, suggestions for tackling difficult situations, and knowing you are improving. This is time well spent.

*Derive happiness in oneself
from a good day's work,
from illuminating the fog
that surrounds us.*

—HENRI MATISSE

82

Reflect

Do you want to feel good about where you are today? Reflect on where you were five years ago.

Those who have most to do, and are willing to work, will find the most time.

—SAMUEL SMILES

83

Slow down

"We are what we repeatedly do.
Excellence, then, is not an act,
but a habit."

—Aristotle

Slow down today and choose excellence. Pay mindful attention to everything you do, say, think. Make all your results turn out the best you can, just for today.

The best way to do field work is not to come up for air until you're done.

—MARGARET MEAD

84

Just do it

You know that thing you have been putting off? Stop right now and do it.

*When you like your work,
every day is a holiday.*

—FRANK TYGER

85
Turn the tables

Try this today: when someone complains or is critical in some way, turn the conversation around and find the positive. Chances are this shift won't even be noticed, and you'll both walk away feeling better.

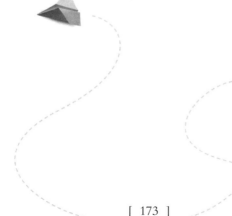

Happiness is the only good.
The time to be happy is now.
The place to be happy
is here. The way to be happy
is to make others so.

—Robert G. Ingersoll

86

Be a mentor

Find someone in your workplace you could help with improving a skill set or working through a problem. Here are some suggestions:

- Make a copy of a relevant magazine article.
- Share an announcement of a workshop.
- Have lunch and ask where a sympathetic ear would be helpful.
- Review that worrisome report; or be a mock audience for the big presentation.
- Teach him or her a software package you know.

Success does not consist of never making blunders, but in never making the same one the second time.

—HENRY WHEELER SHAW
(JOSH BILLINGS)

87

Admit your mistakes

You may think this is the wrong way to gain your coworkers respect, but in fact it is the best way.

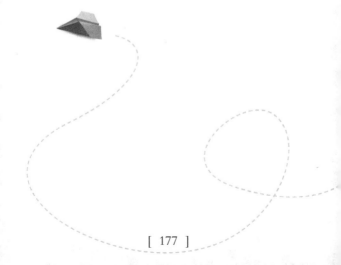

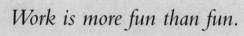

Work is more fun than fun.

—NOEL COWARD

88

Play

We are all little kids in big bodies. Work is just the playground for grown-ups. Take the new guy to lunch. Invite someone who is sitting alone to sit with your group. Introduce yourself to someone you don't know. Tell a coworker he or she is doing a great job.

The first form of happiness is sound health…it is essential to maintain the health of the mind and body simultaneously.

—RIG VEDA

89

Attend to the basics

Don't deny your basic needs. Eat. Drink lots of water. Exercise. Get some air. Take time to rest. Go to bed early tonight. Don't let work dictate these things. Find ways to incorporate these necessary functions into even the busiest schedule.

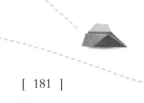

Never continue a job you don't enjoy. If you're happy in what you're doing, you'll like yourself, you'll have inner peace. And if you have that, along with physical health, you will have had more success than you could possibly have imagined.

—ROGER CARAS

90

Look at the big picture

You will find very few policies and practices of your organization were implemented to make you unhappy. Try to see through the eyes of the whole organization.

Relax yourself from one job
by doing a different one.

—ERNEST RENAN

91

Try something different

Albert Einstein's definition of insanity is "to keep doing the same thing over and over again, expecting different results." If you're not getting the results you're after, why not try a different way?

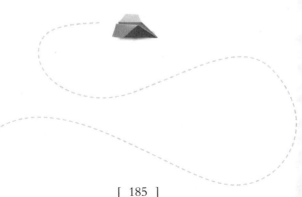

Sometimes when we are generous in small, barely detectable ways it can change someone else's life forever.

—MARGARET CHO

92

A word of thanks

What has your boss done for you lately? How about saying "Thank you"? You may be delighted at the reaction.

In dealings between man and man, truth, sincerity and integrity, are of the utmost importance to the felicity of life.

—Benjamin Franklin

93

Actually use the Golden Rule

Relationship building starts today! Try using the Golden Rule in building up a relationship with a coworker. What is one step that person could take to make things better with you? Now go over and do that very thing.

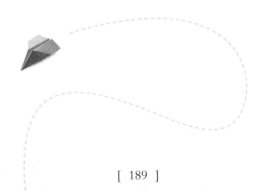

Blessed is he who has found his work; let him ask no other blessedness.

—THOMAS CARLYLE

94

Countdown

Count your blessings. Don't stop until you find at least ten.

Before you agree to do anything that might add even the smallest amount of stress to your life, ask yourself: What is my truest intention? Give yourself time to let a yes resound within you. When it's right, I guarantee that your entire body will feel it.

—OPRAH WINFREY

95

Just say no

Are you feeling overwhelmed? Are you able to confidently say "no" when you are being pushed? Think of someone who recently told you it wasn't possible to do something you asked, or someone you would never dream of asking for a favor. Why do you think this is? Chances are, this person knows how to set limits, and you respect that.

If you set your limits and express yourself kindly and clearly, people won't view you as uncooperative, just in control of yourself. Try it and see!

Sometimes creativity just means the daily work of helping others to see a problem in a different way.

—JOSEPH BADARACCO

96

Reach out

Call that person you have been neglecting or want to get to know better and make plans to meet. Don't worry about being rejected, or that this is "too little, too late." Just do it. It will be appreciated.

Work is the greatest thing in the world, so we should always save some of it for tomorrow.

—DON HEROLD

97
Don't get overworked

If your workload is surpassing your ability to handle it, ask your boss for advice on reprioritizing or managing the extra work.

You'll get one of two results:

1) Some good ideas on getting organized or reshuffling things you had given too much importance; or

2) A lightening of your load, because the boss will have a full understanding of your commitments.

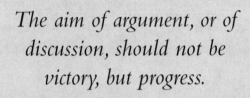

The aim of argument, or of discussion, should not be victory, but progress.

—Joseph Joubert

98

It takes two

Resist the incredible need to be right. Most of our conflict and tension in relationships stems from this mind-set. Just for today, try opening up to others' way of seeing things. When you hear yourself defending your position, stop and consider the other side.

*I'm a great believer in luck,
and I find the harder I
work the more I have of it.*

—THOMAS JEFFERSON

99

See your own strength

Find two things in this job where you have really shown remarkable power. Is it a specific skill? Handling a difficult person well? Meeting deadlines and being accurate? Realize this isn't luck. You have many strengths.

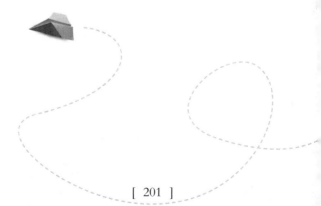

*Reading is to the mind
what exercise is to the body.*

—Sir Richard Steele

100

Take a mental vacation

Reading is one of the best ways to take yourself out of your day-to-day world and escape for awhile. Go out and get that book you have been really wanting to read. No time? Try reading it during lunch, while standing in line, or a couple of pages before bed. This doesn't work with trade journals or newspapers. Read a good book.

Success consists of a series of little daily victories.

—Laddie F. Hutar

101

List your accomplishments

Make a list of all the things you have accomplished in the past year. There are at least seven. Reflect on how productive you really have been, and how many great days you've had. Make today another one.

About the author

Stephanie Goddard Davidson specializes in communication and interpersonal skills training. Her customers include such nationally recognized companies as MCI, BellSouth, Nextel, and Rollins Protective Services.

She is also a nationally certified trainer for Covey's Seven Habits of Highly Effective People, Ridge's People Skills for Managers and Individual Contributors, Myers-Briggs Type Indicator, FranklinCovey's Project Management, and master certified in Achieve Global's Management Programs; as well as an instructor with the American Management Association.

For articles and other useful information, please visit Stephanie's website at http://101-ways-great-day-at-work.com.